NUTRITION AND
YOUR BODY

# YOUR
# BODY ON
# DAIRY

BY CAROLYN WILLIAMS-NOREN

CONTENT CONSULTANT
Nancy Buckley
Instructor, Agricultural, Food & Life Sciences
University of Arkansas

Core Library

An Imprint of Abdo Publishing
abdobooks.com

Cover image:

abdocorelibrary.com

Published by Abdo Publishing, a division of ABDO, PO Box 398166,
Minneapolis, Minnesota 55439. Copyright © 2020 by Abdo Consulting
Group, Inc. International copyrights reserved in all countries. No part of this
book may be reproduced in any form without written permission from the
publisher. Core Library™ is a trademark and logo of Abdo Publishing.

Printed in the United States of America, North Mankato, Minnesota
032019
092019

Cover Photo: Shutterstock Images
Interior Photos: Shutterstock Images, 1, 4–5, 11, 12, 14–15, 22, 24–25, 38–39, 43; Monkey
Business Images/iStockphoto, 6–7; Christian Musat/Shutterstock Images, 9, 45; Eye of Science/
Science Source, 16; Scimat/Science Source, 19, 26; Sergey Tinyakov/Shutterstock Images, 28;
David Pollack/Corbis/Corbis Historical/Getty Images, 32–33; Rob Hainer/Shutterstock Images, 35

Editor: Marie Pearson
Series Designer: Claire Vanden Branden

Library of Congress Control Number: 2018966067

Publisher's Cataloging-in-Publication Data

Names: Williams-Noren, Carolyn, author.
Title: Your body on dairy / by Carolyn Williams-Noren
Description: Minneapolis, Minnesota: Abdo Publishing, 2020 | Series: Nutrition and your body |
    Includes online resources and index.
Identifiers: ISBN 9781532118845 (lib. bdg.) | ISBN 9781532173028 (ebook) | ISBN
    9781644940754 (pbk.)
Subjects: LCSH: Calcium in human nutrition--Juvenile literature. | Dairy products in human
    nutrition--Juvenile literature. | Milk consumption--Juvenile literature. | Food--Health
    aspects--Juvenile literature.
Classification: DDC 613.20--dc23

# CONTENTS

CHAPTER
# ONE

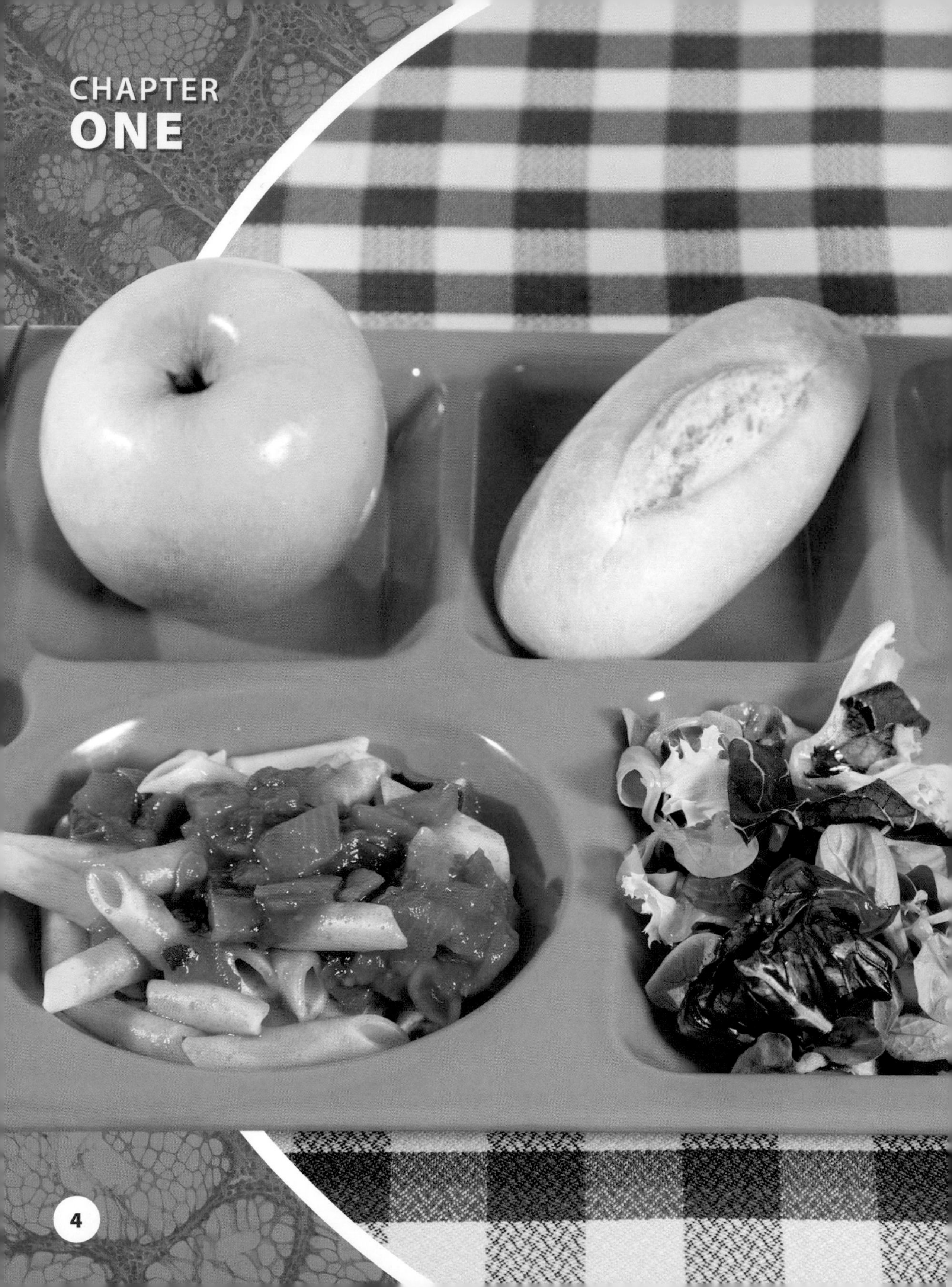

# WHAT IS DAIRY?

The lunchroom fills with fifth graders. The smell of delicious food fills the air. Some kids go right to the tables. They open their lunch bags and start eating. Some kids wait in line for school lunch. One by one, they collect trays full of food. Before sitting down, almost every kid picks up a small, rectangular white carton of milk.

At her table, Janie opens her carton. She folds open the cardboard top. Then she drinks a big gulp of milk. It is refreshing. The milk is cold, slightly sweet, and a little creamy.

Janie keeps sipping the milk in between bites of her lunch. When she's finished eating,

Many schools have milk available at lunch.

Milk has nutrients the body can use for energy.

the carton is empty. The milk is on its way through her digestive system.

After eating, Janie goes outside for recess. She runs around with her friends. Then, Janie goes back to the classroom. All the while, her body is breaking down the milk she drank. Janie's stomach and intestines break the milk into tiny parts her body can use.

Some parts are sugars. The sugar in milk is called lactose. It gives Janie energy right away. It powers her muscles, helping her run, climb, and jump on the playground. Milk's fats and proteins come in bigger pieces. They take longer to digest. Her body uses this energy later in the day. Other parts of the milk, including calcium, will become part of Janie's muscles, bones, brain, and skin as she grows.

## RUMINANTS MAKE IT HAPPEN

All mammals make milk. But humans don't drink dog, cat, or mouse milk. All over the world, people milk cows, sheep, yaks, goats, and camels. These animals are ruminants. Ruminants have strong digestive systems. Their multipart stomachs can break down tough foods such as dry grasses. In the past, some communities went through seasons of little food. But ruminants could eat the dry, tough grasses. The communities relied on the ruminants' milk to survive in places where they couldn't otherwise find food.

## WHERE DOES DAIRY COME FROM?

Female cows, goats, sheep, and other mammals make milk for their babies. Baby mammals—calves, lambs, and human babies—drink milk from their mothers' bodies. When mammal babies are very young, milk from their mothers is the only food they need.

People also drink animals' milk. And people use milk to make foods such as cheese, yogurt, and butter. Milk and foods made from milk are

All mammals need milk when they are young.

called dairy products or dairy foods. Cheese, yogurt, and butter are also dairy products. In the United States, 97 percent of dairy products come from cows. But all foods made from mammals' milk are called dairy products.

## NOT TRUE MILK

Some people drink almond milk, soy milk, oat milk, hemp milk, rice milk, and others. These types of milk are plant based. They're made from grains, seeds, and nuts. These materials are soaked, squeezed, and strained to make the milk. People use plant milks in many of the same ways they use cow's milk. They may put almond milk on cereal. They may mix hemp milk into bread dough or cake batter. But these types of milk aren't dairy products. They didn't come from mammals.

## NOT JUST COWS

In the United States, dairy products from sheep and goats are not as popular as those from cows. But they can be found at many stores. Feta cheese is usually made from sheep's milk. Chèvre is a popular tangy cheese made from goat's milk.

In some parts of the world, people use other animals' milk much more. In the mountains of Nepal, people flavor tea with butter made from yak's milk. In Somalia, people

Americans are used to cow's milk. But many people enjoy milk from other animals too.

# DAIRY PRODUCTS AROUND THE WORLD

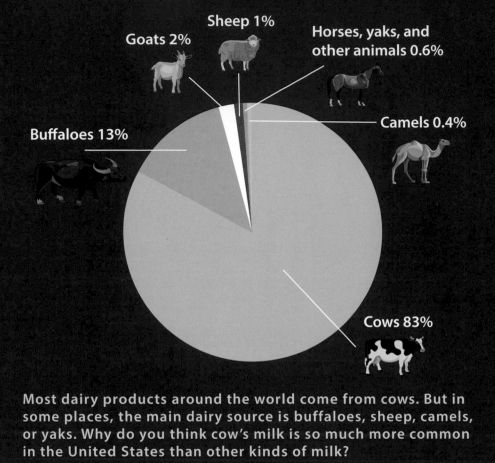

Sheep 1%

Goats 2%

Horses, yaks, and other animals 0.6%

Camels 0.4%

Buffaloes 13%

Cows 83%

Most dairy products around the world come from cows. But in some places, the main dairy source is buffaloes, sheep, camels, or yaks. Why do you think cow's milk is so much more common in the United States than other kinds of milk?

enjoy warm milk fresh from a camel. In Italy, some pizza is topped with cheese made from water buffalo milk. Milk from different animals has slightly different amounts of nutrients. It tastes a bit different.

# YOUR BODY ON DAIRY

For some people, dairy products can be an important part of healthy eating. Some nutrition experts say consuming two or three servings of dairy each day is a good idea. Milk contains protein, fat, and vitamins that the body can use. But dairy isn't the right fit for everyone's bodies. As part of a healthy diet, people should learn about dairy and how it interacts with the body.

## FURTHER EVIDENCE

Chapter One talks about dairy products and how they are used around the world. What was one of the main points of the chapter? What evidence does the author give to support the point? The website below shows how food habits differ in different countries. Does the information on the website support the main point of the chapter? Does it present new evidence?

NATIONAL GEOGRAPHIC: WHAT THE WORLD EATS
abdocorelibrary.com/dairy

# CHAPTER TWO

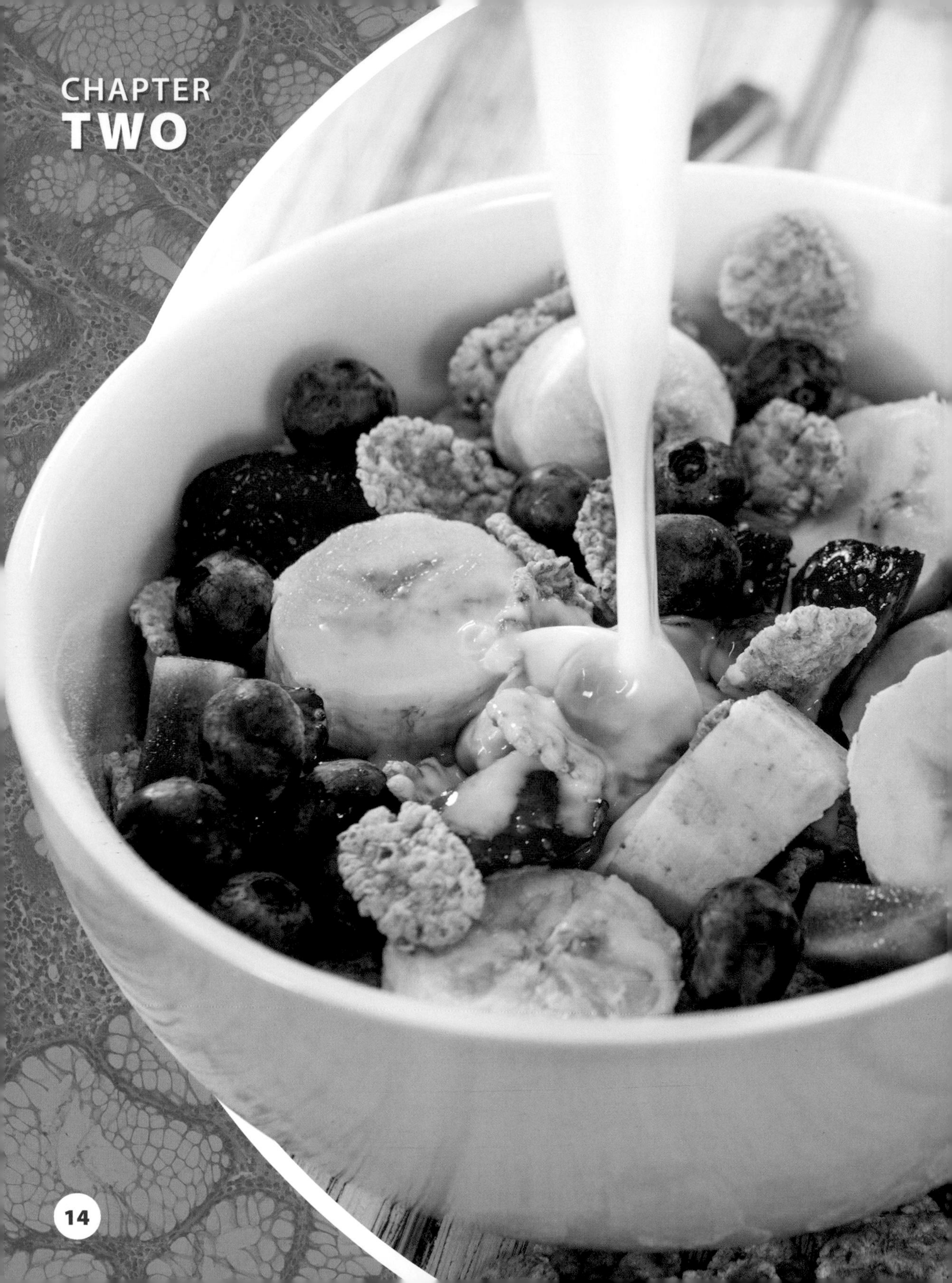

# WHAT'S IN MILK?

Milk is made of many tiny parts mixed together. The body uses each part differently. The majority of cow's milk is water. Water makes up 87.3 percent of a glass of milk. People must drink water to live. It helps the blood carry oxygen and nutrients around the body. It helps the digestive system work well. It protects organs and helps the body stay at a healthy temperature. Most people need about four to six cups of water each day. The water in milk counts toward that total.

Milk can be enjoyed alone or added to other foods and drinks.

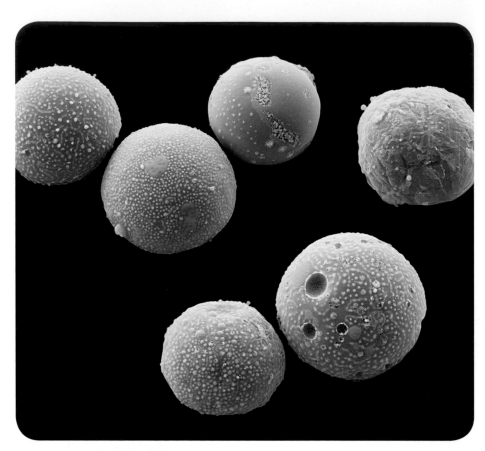

Magnification shows that substances such as proteins stick to fat droplets' skins.

## FAT

Whole cow's milk is 3.9 percent fat. Sometimes dairy companies take some fat out of the milk. It's sold with 1 percent or 2 percent fat. Skim milk has close to zero fat.

Fat floats throughout milk in droplets. The droplets are so tiny people can't see them. Each droplet has a kind of skin around it. The skins keep the droplets separate from each other.

Fat helps the body take in vitamins. It's a good source of energy. And it helps cells, nerves, and muscles work correctly. For a long time, people thought the type of fat in milk was likely to cause heart attacks. But some studies have shown that it may not be harmful in moderation.

## PROTEIN

Nobody can live without protein. The body is made of cells, and cells are made of protein. Protein helps cells grow, work, and stay healthy. A little more than 3 percent of milk is made of protein. There are many types

## WHY IS MILK WHITE?

Each fat droplet in milk has a skin that holds it together. Because of the way light bounces off the skins, the milk looks white. Milk with less fat has a less intense white color. That's because there are fewer fat droplets to scatter the light. Fat also gives milk most of its flavor and odor.

of protein. Each type has its own shape with many folds and twists.

Each type of protein has a special job in the body. Some proteins are the building blocks of organs, muscles, and skin. Some are messengers, sending signals between different parts of the body. Some are enzymes, making cells' work possible. Some proteins carry other molecules throughout the body.

There are dozens of types of protein in milk. They can be sorted into two groups. They are curd proteins and whey proteins.

Whey proteins in milk float around by themselves. Curd proteins stick together in bundles. Each bundle is made of approximately 1,000 proteins. But the bundles are too small to see. Each protein in the bundle has a special job. Some stick to one another. Others cling to the outside of the bundle and keep it from sticking to other nearby bundles.

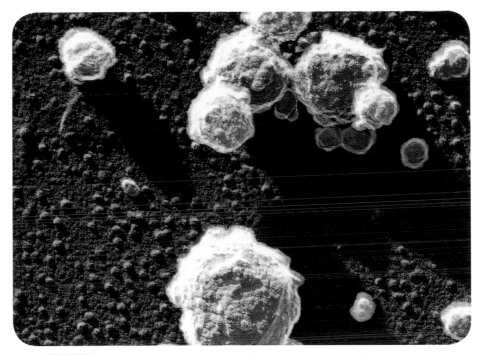

Curd protein bundles are also called casein micelles.

## LACTOSE

Lactose makes up 4.6 percent of milk. Forty percent of milk's calories come from this sugar. Lactose is in every animal's milk.

Sugars such as lactose are naturally found in many foods. These sugars are one of the main sources of fuel and energy for our bodies. But nutrition experts say people should not have too much sugar. Eating a lot of sugar at once is hard on the body. Too much sugar in

# WHAT MILK IS MADE OF

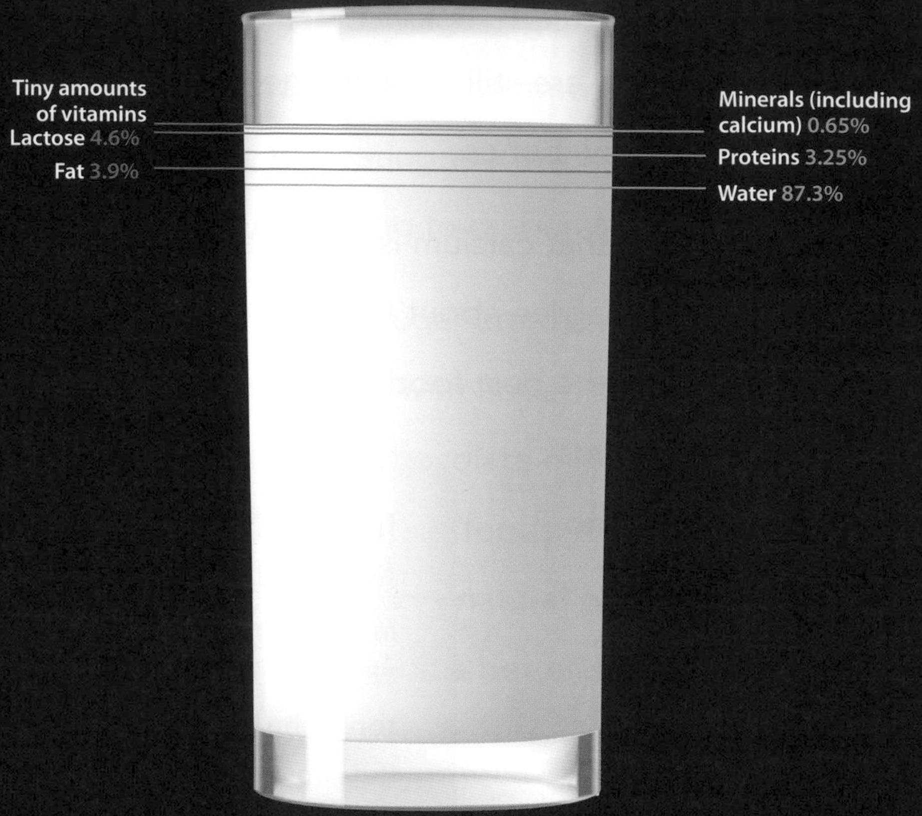

Tiny amounts
of vitamins
Lactose 4.6%

Fat 3.9%

Minerals (including
calcium) 0.65%

Proteins 3.25%

Water 87.3%

Every glass of whole cow's milk contains the same mix of nutrients. Our bodies use each part of the milk differently. Does anything about the mix of nutrients in milk surprise you? Ask a friend who hasn't seen this illustration to make a guess about how much water, fat, sugar, and protein are in milk. Was your friend right?

Dairy companies also add vitamin D to most milk. Vitamin D is both important and hard to get. It isn't in many foods. The human body makes vitamin D when the skin is exposed to sun. But to make enough, people need plenty of sun. Some people don't get enough sunlight. They may work long hours indoors. Or they may live in cold or cloudy places. Without vitamin D, the body can't absorb calcium.

By adding vitamin D to milk, dairy companies are trying to make sure people have enough of both nutrients to stay healthy. Calcium and vitamin D are important for strong bone health. But a study in 2014 found that adding extra vitamin D may not be needed for bone strength.

## EXPLORE ONLINE

Chapter Two discusses protein. Visit the website below to find out more about protein. How is the information on the website the same as the information in Chapter Two? What new facts about protein did you learn from the website?

KIDSHEALTH: LEARNING ABOUT PROTEINS
abdocorelibrary.com/dairy

CHAPTER
# THREE

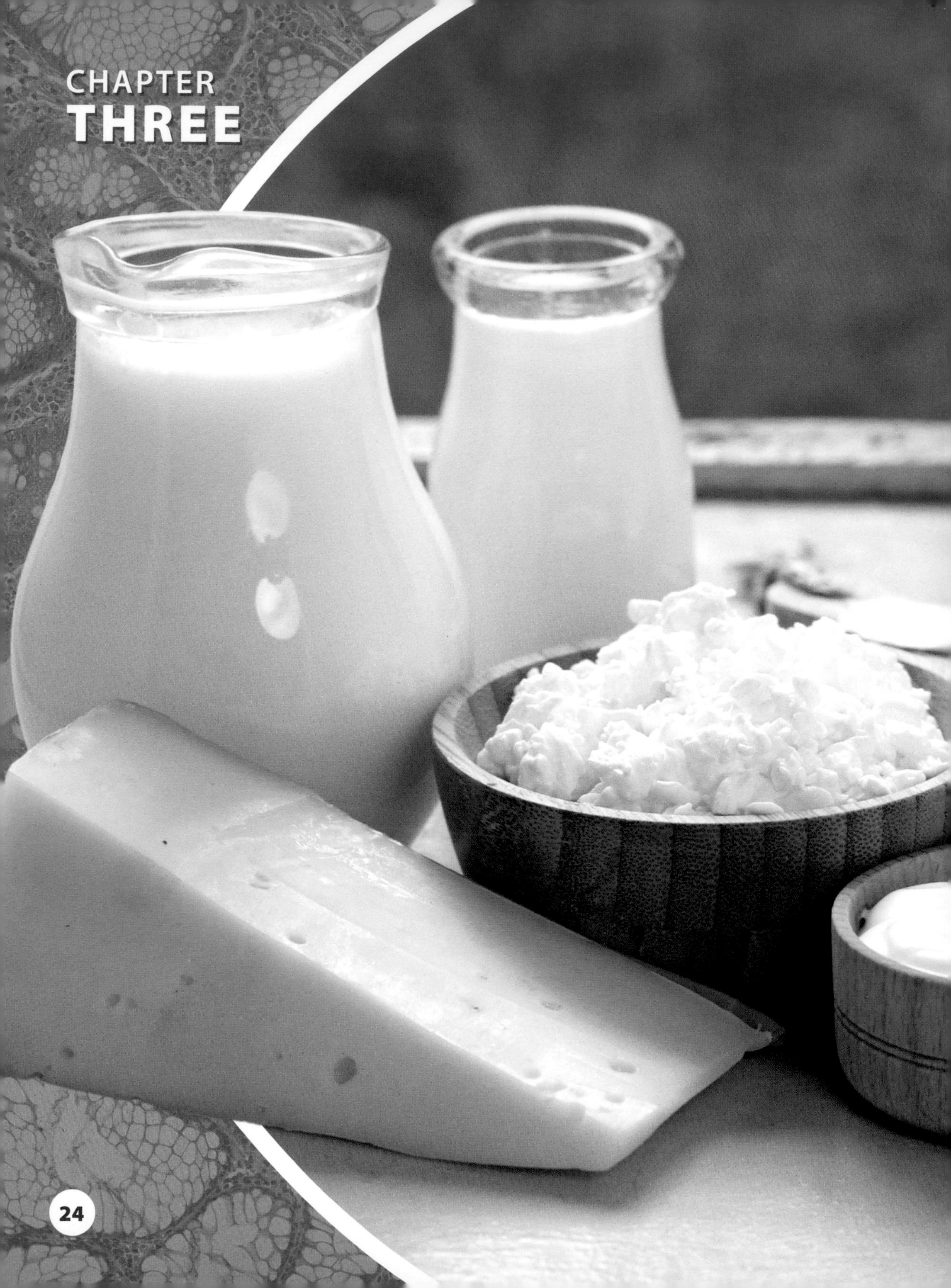

# OTHER DAIRY FOODS

A block of cheese, a tub of yogurt, and a package of butter have different colors, textures, and tastes. But milk is the number one ingredient. With just a little work, sweet, smooth, white milk becomes firm cheese, tangy yogurt, or golden butter.

## YOGURT

Bacteria turn milk into yogurt. Bacteria are too small for the human eye to see. Each is just one cell. Bacteria are everywhere. They're on skin, inside the body, in water, and on every surface.

Dairy products come in a variety of textures, from liquids to solids.

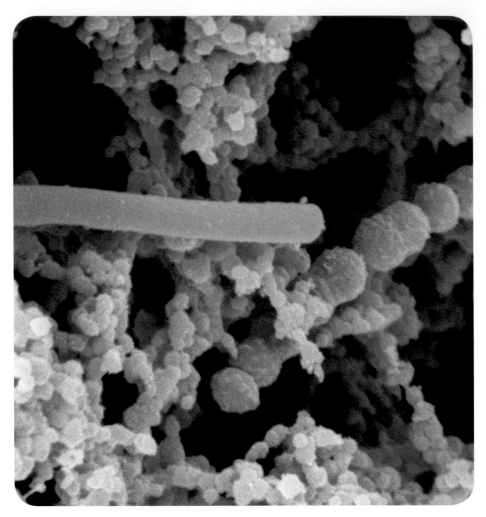

Lactic acid bacteria, *blue and red*, help make yogurt.

Bacteria eat sugar, but most can't break down lactose. However, one special group of bacteria, called lactic acid bacteria, can. When lactic acid bacteria are added to milk, they eat the lactose. The bacteria use some parts of the lactose for energy.

But one part of the lactose isn't useful for the bacteria. The bacteria leave this part behind. This part is called lactic acid. The lactic acid changes the milk. It makes it more difficult for other kinds of bacteria to live in the milk. It also changes the proteins in the milk. It makes the calcium glue that holds the curd proteins together less sticky. The protein bundles fall apart and unfold.

Then the proteins stick to each other again. But the lactic acid makes them stick together differently. They don't form bundles. Instead, they make one big, soft mesh of proteins. Water and fats are trapped inside the mesh. This creates the thick, creamy texture of yogurt.

Like milk, yogurt is a source of protein and calcium. And it can be full fat, low fat, or no fat, depending on what type of milk is used to make it. But eating yogurt affects the body a little differently than drinking milk does. When people eat yogurt, they also take in lactic

Curds are pressed into molds to make blocks of cheese.

acid bacteria. Lactic acid bacteria can help the body fight bacteria that make people sick.

Plain yogurt also has less sugar than milk. That's because the lactic acid bacteria have eaten some of the milk's lactose in the process of making the yogurt. But some flavored yogurts have a lot of added sugar. So be careful to eat those in moderation. Or enjoy plain yogurt with fresh fruit.

## CHEESE

Cheese is made from milk and lactic acid bacteria too. But cheese owes its special texture to one more key ingredient called rennet. Rennet is a type of protein. It breaks off the outsides of the curd protein bundles so the bundles no longer push each other away. They stick together in firm shapes called curds. Squeezed together, the curds become cheese. A liquid called whey, made of whey proteins and water, is left behind.

### FINDING RENNET

People first found rennet in calves' stomachs. Rennet helps calves digest milk. Today, people typically manufacture rennet. This human-made version is sometimes called vegetable rennet. But some cheeses, including many made in Europe, are still made with rennet from calves' stomachs.

Cheese has many of the same vitamins as milk does. But there are also some big differences between a slice of cheese and a cup of milk. There is less lactose in cheese. A bit of the protein is taken away. The end result is made mostly of protein and fat. It's richer in calories than milk is. One serving of cheese is much smaller than one serving of milk.

# BUTTER

Cheese and milk rely on protein for their taste and texture, but butter is all about fat. Making butter begins with cream. Cream is made of just the fattiest parts of milk. In raw, unprocessed milk, fat droplets will float slowly to the top. These form the cream. After some time, the cream can be skimmed off, leaving lower-fat milk behind.

## SO MANY CHEESES!

There are many types of cheese. A small change in any of the basic cheese-making steps can make a big difference in flavor and texture. Some things that influence these differences include the animal the milk comes from, the type of rennet used, and how much water is squeezed out of the curds.

Butter is almost all fat. It doesn't include milk's calcium, protein, sugars, or water. It does have some vitamins. But butter is a high-calorie food. It's good to eat it in small amounts alongside other foods that offer more nutrients.

# STRAIGHT TO THE
# SOURCE

Italian explorer Marco Polo wrote the following passage more than 800 years ago. He describes a dairy food eaten by the Tartar people in what is now Russia:

*[The Tartar armies] make provisions also of milk, thickened or dried to the state of a hard paste, which they prepare in the following manner. They boil the milk, and skimming off the rich or creamy part as it rises to the top, put it into a separate vessel as butter; for so long as that remains in the milk, it will not become hard. The milk is then exposed to the sun until it dries. [When it is to be used,] some is put into a bottle with as much water as is thought necessary. By their motion in riding, the contents are violently shaken, and a thin porridge is produced, upon which they make their dinner.*

Source: Harold McGee. *On Food and Cooking*. New York: Scribner, 2004. Print. 23.

## Consider Your Audience

Read the passage closely. Consider how you would adapt it for a different audience, such as your parents or friends. Write a blog post conveying this same information for the new audience. Write it so that it can be understood by them. How does your new approach differ from the original text, and why?

Drink M
Every Da

# IS DAIRY FOR EVERYONE?

For a long time, dairy companies have advertised cow's milk as one of the very best foods for building strong bones and good health. And milk does contain protein, fat, calcium, and vitamins that human bodies need. But science hasn't proven that drinking milk is the only or best way to get these nutrients.

There is some good evidence that milk is important to kids' bone strength. But other studies find that milk doesn't really strengthen bones in the long run. And some studies find a connection between drinking large amounts of milk and a higher risk of certain cancers.

Advertisements have promoted milk since the 1930s.

US government scientists publish guidelines about which types of foods to eat. They're called the MyPlate guidelines. They say that, for most people, it's a good idea to eat two to three servings of low-fat or fat-free milk or yogurt daily.

Scientists at Harvard University have made a different set of guidelines. It's called the Healthy Eating Plate. It says one to two servings of dairy per day is enough. More dairy than that may increase the risk of some cancers.

The high amounts of fat in some dairy foods may lead to heart disease. But scientists don't yet understand everything about how dairy foods affect people.

Eating dairy is a convenient and affordable way to get many important nutrients. But all of these nutrients can be found in other foods too. Leafy green vegetables have calcium. But people have to eat a lot more of these foods to get the same amount they would in dairy foods. Soy milk often has

Some soy milks have calcium, protein, and other nutrients added to them.

04 16 15 03:01 12-11 EH2 A

50% MORE CALCIUM
THAN DAIRY MILK*

NO ARTIFICIAL COLORS, FLAVORS OR SWEETENERS

NO LACTOSE, DAIRY, GLUTEN OR CHOLESTEROL

good source of
Plant-Powered
PROTEIN

*Silk*®
ORIGINAL
SOYMILK

HEART
HEALTHY
PROTEIN

Nutritionista's Delight

1 cup Silk® soymilk
1 cup frozen fruit
1/2 cup baby kale or spinach
1/4 avocado
1 Tbsp cocoa powder

Blend until smooth. Yummy with tart cherries, pineapple or berries.

Good source of protein!

Find more great recipes at Silk.com

Put a little ♥ in your day

In a glass, over cereal or in a smoothie, our soymilk is pure bliss guaranteed. And if you don't agree, we'll give your money back. Promise.

Love It Guarantee
OR YOUR MONEY BACK

NON GMO Project
VERIFIED
nongmoproject.org

*As part of a diet low in saturated fat and cholesterol, 25g soy protein per day may reduce the risk of heart disease. This product has 8g/serv.

1/2 F. GALLON (1.89

added calcium. Some cereals have added calcium. Meats, fish, grains, and legumes have protein. Fruits, vegetables, and other types of whole, natural foods have many vitamins.

## WHEN MILK MAKES YOU SICK

Some people feel fine after drinking milk. But that's only true for approximately 35 percent of the world. Most older kids and adults don't feel very well after drinking milk. This can be due to lactose intolerance.

To use lactose, the body needs to break it apart. The way to do that is with a special protein called lactase. Babies' bodies make plenty of lactase. The bodies of some kids and adults do too. But, by age five, most people's bodies don't make much lactase at all. Without lactase, the small intestine can't break down the sugar in milk. So the sugar moves along into the large intestine, where it causes gas, diarrhea, and pain.

Most lactose intolerance is hereditary. It's passed down from a person's parents. Lactose intolerance is more common in some parts of the world than in others. Almost all Native American and Asian people are lactose intolerant. Most people with northern European ancestry can drink milk just fine. Among people with ancestors from Latin America or Africa, the likelihood falls in between.

People who are lactose intolerant can sometimes drink small amounts of milk without feeling sick. And some other dairy foods have less lactose than plain milk does. Yogurt and cheese have much less lactose. So people who have trouble

## MILK WITHOUT THE MOO?

Perfect Day, a company based in California, is finding a way to make cow's milk without cows. Using yeast, sugar, genes, and 3-D printing, they can build curd proteins and whey proteins exactly like those found in cow's milk. This uses much less land, water, and energy than dairy farming. Perfect Day's milk is also lactose free. When it's ready to sell, it might be a good solution for people who want dairy products without dairy's impact on nature.

People with lactose intolerance can often eat aged cheeses such as cheddar.

with lactose often don't have trouble with yogurt and certain cheeses.

## ALLERGIES

Some people avoid dairy for other reasons. Some are allergic to milk. A milk allergy is different from lactose intolerance. In an allergy, the immune system

reacts to the proteins in milk. A milk allergy can cause a runny nose or watery eyes. It can also cause more serious problems. It can make a person vomit or have trouble breathing.

Milk allergies are much less common than lactose intolerance. Approximately 3 percent of children are allergic to milk. Many people outgrow the allergy as they get older. But some people stay allergic to milk for their whole lives.

## CAREFUL CHOICES

When people don't eat dairy products, they have to choose other foods carefully. They need to make sure they get enough nutrients from other foods. Many people around the world eat a healthy diet that contains little or no dairy. People who do eat dairy products also need to make careful food choices. They need to take care not to rely too much on dairy foods.

Lactose intolerance and milk allergies can cause people to avoid dairy. People who don't have a reaction to dairy must think of how dairy fits into their lives. Doctors can help them choose foods that keep them healthy. For some people, dairy is one of the many foods they rely on to get the nutrients they need.

# STRAIGHT TO THE
# SOURCE

The Harvard T. H. Chan School of Public Health explains why dairy is best in moderation:

> *Currently, there's no good evidence that consuming more than one serving of milk per day in addition to a reasonable diet . . . will reduce fracture risk. Because of unresolved concerns about the risk of ovarian and prostate cancer, it may be prudent to avoid higher intakes of dairy products.*
>
> *At moderate levels, though, consumption of calcium and dairy products has benefits beyond bone health, including possibly lowering the risk of . . . colon cancer. . . . Most of the [protection against colon cancer] comes from having just one or maybe two glasses of milk per day in addition to what we get from other foods in our diet.*
>
> Source: "Calcium: What's Best for Your Bones and Health?" *Harvard T. H. Chan School of Public Health*. Harvard College, 2019. Web. Accessed January 29, 2019.

## Back It Up

The author of this text is using evidence to support a point. Write a paragraph describing the point the author is making and two or three pieces of evidence the author uses to make the point.

# FAST FACTS

- Dairy products are foods made from the milk of mammals.

- Most dairy products in the United States are made from cow's milk.

- Milk use varies in different parts of the world. Some people use milk from goats, sheep, buffaloes, yaks, and camels, and other people use few or no dairy products.

- The main parts of milk are water, protein, fat, sugar, vitamins, and calcium.

- Some common dairy products are yogurt, cheese, and butter.

- Yogurt and cheese have less lactose than milk.

- Butter and cheese are high in fat.

- Milk gives people many important nutrients, but it isn't the only way to get those nutrients.

- Lactose intolerance means not being able to digest lactose, the sugar in milk. Many people are lactose intolerant and feel sick after drinking too much milk.

- Milk allergies are caused by a person's immune system reacting to milk's proteins.

- It is possible for people to get all the nutrients they need without dairy.

- Whether or not people consume dairy, it's important to choose foods that have plenty of calcium and protein and to eat high-fat, high-calorie, and high-sugar foods in moderation.

# STOP AND THINK

## Say What?

Learning about dairy and nutrition can mean learning a lot of new words. Find five words in this book that you've never heard before. Use a dictionary to find out what they mean. Then write the meanings in your own words. Try using each word in a new sentence.

## Why Do I Care?

Maybe you don't feel sick after eating dairy products. That doesn't mean you can't think about how dairy affects your body. How does your body use the nutrients in dairy? What choices do you make about dairy products? Now that you've learned more about dairy products in this book, are there food choices or habits that you'd like to change?

## Surprise Me

Chapter Three describes how milk is used to make a variety of dairy products. Which facts in this chapter were most surprising to you? Write a few sentences about each fact. Why did you find each fact surprising?

## Another View

This book talks about the importance of moderation in choosing foods, including dairy products. As you know, every source is different. Ask a librarian or another adult to help you find another source about dairy products. Compare and contrast the new source's point of view with that of this book's author. What is the point of view of each author? How are they similar and why? How are they different and why?

# GLOSSARY

**ancestors**
a person's great-grandparents and the relatives who came before them

**calorie**
a unit that measures the amount of energy a food produces when it's taken into the body

**digestive system**
a group of organs that work together to turn food into fuel for the body

**gene**
the part of DNA that passes on from parents to offspring and controls traits such as hair color and height

**intestines**
the organs in the digestive system after the stomach that take in nutrients and water and create waste

**intolerance**
the state of being unable to pass something through the body without suffering a reaction

**moderation**
the act of avoiding extreme highs and lows

**molecule**
the smallest unit of a chemical compound

**nutrient**
something in food that helps people, animals, and plants live and grow

# ONLINE RESOURCES

To learn more about your body on dairy, visit our free resource websites below.

### Core Library
### CONNECTION
FREE! COMMON CORE MULTIMEDIA RESOURCES

Visit **abdocorelibrary.com** or scan this QR code for free Common Core resources for teachers and students, including vetted activities, multimedia, and booklinks, for deeper subject comprehension.

### Booklinks
### NONFICTION NETWORK
FREE! ONLINE NONFICTION RESOURCES

Visit **abdobooklinks.com** or scan this QR code for free additional online weblinks for further learning. These links are routinely monitored and updated to provide the most current information available.

# LEARN MORE

Lusted, Marcia Amidon. *Gluten-Free and Other Special Diets*. Minneapolis, MN: Abdo Publishing, 2016. Print.

Reinke, Beth Bence. *Nutrition Basics*. Minneapolis, MN: Abdo Publishing, 2016. Print.

# INDEX

## About the Author

Carolyn Williams-Noren writes poems and lyric essays in addition to nonfiction books for young people. She ate a lot of cheddar cheese while writing this book. She lives in Minneapolis with her husband and two daughters.